Keep T.... ~cui Hot!

Your Business Solution Guide for
Operating and Growing Your Barber Shop
Volume II

Alan D. Benson, MBA, MPA

Foreword by Donte' L. Jones
Beyond the Cut Barber Shop LLC

MHB Publishing
101 North 7th Street
Louisville, KY 40202
alandbenson.com

Keep That Seat Hot!

Your Business Solution Guide for
Operating and Growing Your Barber Shop
Volume II

Foreword by Donte' L. Jones
Beyond the Cut Barber Shop LLC

When I was seven, my grandfather would take me over to Hinkle's Barber Shop in the Big A Shopping Center in Louisville, Kentucky. I would love the smell of that aftershave he put on me after every cut. It made me feel like a man and part of the crew. Hinkle attracted many people, both the fellas from neighborhoods, and local celebrities like University of Louisville basketball greats Darrell Griffith, Charles Jones, Scooter and Rodney McCray, and the Greatest of All Time (GOAT), Muhammad Ali. The smell of the aftershave and being in that atmosphere made me feel like the barber shop was the place to be.

At the age of 14, my girlfriend bought me a pair of clippers, and, for about a year, I would experiment on myself and my brother. After about a year, I had a porch full of people wanting to get their hair cut. I didn't charge money, but rather a bag of chips and a pop. My mother also would tell me the utility bill increased because of my cutting. It was not until my girlfriend moved across town that I started charging $1 to $2 because I needed bus fare. As I saw it, cutting hair was something I would just do.

I would cut hair, but I never thought it would be a way of

making a living. I would try various entrepreneurial ventures, but never barbering. I participated in network marketing and joined groups. It then became apparent to me while employed at Tumbleweed, I made more money cutting hair in two days than what I made in a full week at Tumbleweed. My desire to own my own business continued and even grew stronger. I researched more books on business and self-development.

For more than five years I continued to pursue business ventures that weren't for me. Then that glaring light in my mind went off again when I ran into a friend whom I'd taught to cut hair. He talked about *the life* and days past, and at the end of our conversation my friend said we needed to stay in touch. He gave me his business card. His card showed he was a licensed barber, and that made me question, "Why am I not a barber?" So, I enrolled in barber school. When I enrolled, I was thinking about making more income to have freedom and to make my own schedule. After cutting hair for six years, I got that entrepreneurial itch and opened my barber shop. Business went well, and my barbering seat was always hot.

Alan, my childhood friend from Catalpa Street, was one of my clients. When he would stop by, we would laugh, joke, and talk about any and everything. One evening while getting his hair cut, Alan told me that he taught entrepreneurship classes. He noticed some of the students owned salons and barber shops, and based on the questions they were asking him, he posed the question, "Are barbers taught business while going through school?" Alan then asked me if I was taught business strategies and concepts, and further asked if a business book for barbers would better equip them. I felt it was an ingenious idea and much needed for the barbering industry.

Alan wrote his first book on the business of barbering, *Keep That Seat Hot.* The book was very beneficial for me because it discussed business strategies that enhanced me in terms of looking at what I do and looking at it as a business. Having the business paperwork in place, for example. I began to look at my business through a different lens. The book gave me the tools to offer better customer service, and because of the tools I used from his book, it had a direct impact on my business. My business has grown from one barber shop to two, with two beauty salons.

Alan and I talk often, and with Volume II of *Keep That Seat Hot*, I highly recommend this book to barbers, because the barbering industry is evolving with more competition and more special services for customers. Barbers need the skillset and education to offer special services, and they need business savvy to attract more customers. *Keep That Seat Hot Volume II* will give you the business know-how to attract those customers and grow your business. It is a must read!

Table of Contents

Dedication

I dedicate this book to my Mom, Marthella H. Benson. Your love, encouragement, and level of accountability have made me who I am today. For that, your teachings shall continue to guide my thoughts in my daily journey.

Preface

Thanks for picking up Volume II of Keep that Seat Hot! Since writing my first edition in 2017, a lot has changed, most notably, the pandemic that we are living in. The pandemic has forced a lot of businesses to rethink and strategize the way they operate, attract customers and stay relevant. As Donte Jones, owner of Beyond the Cuts Barber Shop and Salon, stated, "It has forced barbers to be more aware of health and safety protocols, money management, and having financial paperwork in place. We cannot have a barber shop full of customers; we have to set up appointments." Occurrences and incidents, whether positive or negative, are an opportunity for us to evaluate how we are operating, and an opportunity to look at new strategies to beat out the competition. That is why I am still excited about bringing this book to you.

I am passionate about helping others by sharing business strategies and positioning them to be in a better place. I call it my commonsense strategy to assist one to become a better businessperson, business operator, and leader in the barbering industry. This book will serve as a guide to operating a barbering business. Through research, and conversations with barbers, I discovered many schools only teach you the applications of barbering and how to pass the state board, but very little business. Whether you are leasing or own your own barber shop or are a 1099 contract barber, knowing business is awfully important to your livelihood. It will also position you to make more money. Thus, will give you a better quality of life.

So what inspired me to write this book on barbering and to continue with a series? For starters, the barber shop is a part of my life experience. Barber shops have been and still are stable businesses in our society. Barbering is a very respectable profession where barbers can earn a substantial amount of money. Barber shops are a place where men and women come together to laugh, debate, and to relax. I have looked at barber shops through the customer's lenses, and have seen the good, bad, and ugly. I have talked to several barbers about their marketing, their financial future, and their business understanding throughout the years. It is not rocket science. It is about implementing basic practices and sticking to them. At times situations might cause you to make some adjustments, like what we are experiencing now with this pandemic.

You will find this book to be straightforward, easy to understand, and clear in its instructions and examples. The title indicates that when barbers have loyal, repeat customers, their barbering seats will always be hot. When the seat is hot, that means that the barber is making money.

I love going to the barber shop because it is a place where men hang out and laugh. I have had the best times in barber shops. I have heard stories of joy, stories of laughter, and stories of pain. For those reasons alone, I see the barber shop as a healing place for most men and some women.

Acknowledgements

First and foremost, I would like to thank God for giving me the insight, spirit, drive, and knowledge to write this book. Through life I had various experiences, both great and significant, and I can see why I had those experiences, as they helped to shape who I am today. Thank you, God! Secondly, I uplift my mother, Marthella H. Benson, who inspired me beyond belief. She is no longer here with me, but her spirit and teachings live within me. She always pushed me to be a better person and to hold myself accountable. She always dared me to do right.

I also would like to thank my father, Sam D. Benson. He is my hero because he is a man of faith, strength, and achievement. I also thank Carlos. He is a friend, a man filled with history, life wisdom, and a great man of Alpha Phi Alpha Fraternity, Inc. What he has taught me through the years has been lifesaving. Thanks, Frat! I want to thank my barber, Donte, the owner of Beyond the Cuts Barber Shop back home. Donte and I grew up on the same street, and I am thankful for his friendship. I am really proud of his deliberate pursuit in achieving his vision to make his business and community a better place. Since the publication of my first book, he has expanded his business. I would also like to thank my creative designer, Audra Gray. Her attention to detail and ability to make the ordinary extraordinary is like none other. Finally, and not least, I would like to thank my friend and fellow Marine, Chris Goodwin for editing this book as well as Sheryl Edelen. I also thank all those in my life who have had an impact on my life's journey.

Introduction

After publishing the first volume of ***Keep That Seat Hot***, I had the opportunity to speak at different events and meet several people in the barbering industry. I spoke at the national barbering conference, colleges, community events, barbering shows and one-on-one with many barbers. Often I sold my book out of my car, and I really enjoyed that because I heard the stories of so many barbers. I will never forget meeting the barber in Atlanta, GA and him telling me how he put his children through college and acquired several real estate properties. I also was enamored when I met the barber whose place of business looked like a palace. It was so clean and royal. I could have eaten off the floor. Speaking and hearing the stories of barbers gave me a greater appreciation and confirmation that barber shops are one of the cornerstones in the African-American community.

While growing up, I remember going to the barber shop with my father. That experience was always something I enjoyed because as a young man, I would hear all the conversations of the older men. I would listen attentively as they talked about "grown folks" business. My father and his friends would talk about everything, and I am sure it was filtered because the men in that barber shop were about maintaining a high level of respect for themselves. The barber shop was filled with various magazines and books I always enjoyed reading, like *Sports Illustrated, Ebony,* and *Jet Magazine.* Those fond memories have faded, but the congregation and socialization of the barber shop are still present because the barber shop is still a place where men come together to talk about everything. They discuss sports, politics, and much more.

The barber shop is an important element to communities, and some would argue the barber shop is recession-proof; men and women both need and like to get their hair cut and styled. Because of the need, the value it can bring customers and its historical foundation, the barber shop presents many business opportunities if strategically planned and carried out. The business opportunity that a barber shop can offer involves owning and operating a business, selling products in the shop and creating wealth for yourself. It is hard work, but like anything, if you put your time into it, it can be rewarding. Owning a barber shop presents many benefits, and the most important is having the autonomy and freedom of ownership and the opportunity to create wealth.

At the end of each chapter, I have questions I want you to answer. These questions will help you organize your thoughts and execute your plan. Being an owner and operating a business requires some skill, discipline and know-how. It is not hard to do, but to alleviate some headaches, this book will walk you through the necessary steps in owning and operating a barber shop.

With corporations and discount barbering taking away some of the barbering business, I will explain why barbering is still a growth business and what one needs to do to ensure that his or her business grows. For example, having the shop at the right location to create and sustain business growth is essential.

Since we are still living within a pandemic, the first chapter will cover a new way of operating your business. The next chapter covers steps for you to become licensed and how to run an operationally efficient and effective barbering business. I have heard many barbers say, *"I am getting my hustle on with this barbering!"* Your barber shop is not a hustle; rather, it is a great opportunity for you to create an empire.

I will then discuss your barber shop business and having the right people on your team. Having the right people on your team can grow your business just as well as having the wrong people can kill it. I will discuss some things to look for that will better position your business in hiring and highlight things to avoid. What will break the back of any business is nonmanagement and mismanagement of business funds. I will give strategies for maximizing your revenue and ways to control costs. I also will discuss strategies on pricing.

The "If I Build It, They Will Come" section will cover strategies for marketing your barber shop. This is an important section because it will give you tips and suggestions on how to market the products and services in your barber shop. This section will cover the 4Ps of Marketing: Product, Price, Place, and Promotion. Branding your barber shop is very important. Branding is a special logo, a slogan, a name, a product look, or a way of providing service that people will identify only your barber shop as having. Branding is important because it's what differentiates your barber shop from others. For example, when people see the golden arches, they immediately think about McDonald's.

Being your customer's keeper is another important aspect of running a business. In this section, I will discuss customer service in general and how to further provide excellent customer service. The reality is that without customers you will not have a business. I will discuss strategies for getting, keeping, and growing your customer base.

We all remember reading fairy tales where beautiful castles were very precious and appealing to the eye. In this section, I will discuss how having the right curb appeal will attract customers. This is a section that turns into marketing, branding, and overall strategy in maintaining and growing your barber shop.

Using the right technology and planning are critical steps to owning, operating, and growing your barbering business. This chapter tells what technology is available to assist your business in becoming more operationally efficient and what steps to take to turn your barber shop into a corporation of barber shops throughout the city, state or nation.

Chapter 1: A New Way of Operating Your Business

In January 2020 I was asked to give a presentation to the Louisville Chapter of the Society for Human Resources Management on Workplace Safety Disaster Planning and Recovery. I considered it an honor to present, and I was confident in presenting because I had led efforts in that area. I prepared for my presentation according as I do all my talks—focused on engaging the audience by providing useful information.

My preparation for my presentation consisted of doing my research, reflection on how I handled workforce disasters in my professional roles, and asking the question *what if?* During that time I was hearing through the news about the pandemic. The World Health Organization issued a Global Health Emergency on January 31st, and the United States declared a public health emergency on February 3rd. My presentation was scheduled for February 11, 2020. Knowing those were issued, I included it in my presentation, but did not place that much emphasis on it. While I thought it was an issue of importance, I never thought of the magnitude of what could possibly happen and what consequential effect it was going to have on the entire United States and the globe. On March 13th, former President Trump declared *COVID-19* as a National Emergency. That is when everything shut down.

In the first edition of my first book, ***"Keep That Seat Hot,"*** I opened by saying I believe barbering is recession-proof, meaning, regardless of the economy, barbers could still operate on a somewhat consistent basis. Regardless of one's circumstances, they still likely are going to get their hair cut or styled. The pandemic changed everything. It caused practically everything, including barber shops and salons to shut down. There was no cure and people were dying. Because this was the reality, the United States had to act quickly to slow the spread of COVID-19, take care of those affected by it, and keep the economy moving.

The United States moved to save people, but far too many were dying because there was not a true understanding of the cause or a cure. Although a pandemic happened over 100 years ago, the United States and the world were in uncharted territory because of its global impact.

To bring relief, the United States issued checks to US citizens and to businesses. If you owned a business, whether small or large, you could apply for a grant for up to 10,000 dollars, a forgivable loan based on your net income, and a low percentage disaster relief loan. The grant, forgivable loan, and disaster relief loan were administered through the Small Business Administration (SBA). Even while many businesses were receiving relief, I saw that we were in a new form of business. I say it's a new form because, for one, people have not gone back to work, and for two because of the workforce shortages and supplies, the economy has not fully rebounded. So how does that affect the barbering industry? With the workforce shortages, people are leaving their jobs and looking for new career opportunities. One of those opportunities could be people wanting to become barbers. If that is the case, that means that there is more competition within the barbering industry. When there is more competition in any industry, that means those who work within that industry have to put on their creative caps to retain and attract more customers.

Regardless to whether we were living through a pandemic or living pre-pandemic, as business owners we should ALWAYS have a mindset of exploring ways to be the best we can be in our personal life, family, and business. The pandemic merely added an extra layer of complexity to operating your barber shop. It is true that the pandemic had consequential effects on many businesses, both large and small, and this was out of our control. But when you have your business in order, it helps to insulate the blow of any devastation. So, moving forward as a business, please do the following:

- Make sure you have your tax documents up to date and in order. **Note:** Seek a CPA for assistance or someone skilled in that area.

- If you are leasing a building, have an attorney to review

the lease to ensure that it is fair and equitable, and a win-win in your favor.

- Keep track of your cash flow and make deposits to establish a record of what you are making.

- Always research the best alternatives when making business decisions.

- Always seek wise counsel.

- Always remember, if it is too good to be true, it usually is.

Chapter 2: Why Is Barbering Still a Growth and Stable Business?

Barbering has been around for ages, and I believe it is a profession people must have access to, to look their best. Barbers cut, trim, shampoo and style hair, mostly for male customers. They also may fit hairpieces and perform facials. Depending on the state in which they work, some barbers are licensed to color, bleach, highlight hair, and offer permanent wave services (Statistics, 2016). Common tools include combs, scissors, straight razors, and clippers. Outside of a catastrophic pandemic, I feel the barber shop is recession-proof because, despite the economy, people prioritize finding resources to have their hair cut and groomed.

Becoming a barber requires attending barber school and obtaining a license. The requirements to become a barber vary by state, but on average it takes between 1500 and 2000 hours of instruction in a barber school before a person is permitted to sit for the exams.

You also will need to be at least 16 years old, have a high school diploma or GED and pass the appropriate licensing exams. After successful completion of barbering school and licensing, one is on his or her way in the barbering profession.

So why is barbering a growth and stable business venture? The answers are growth in employment, demand for barbers and above-average median income.

Employment and Demands of Barbering

Entering the barbering industry presents many opportunities for growth and wealth. Overall employment and demand for barbers was projected to grow 10 percent from 2014 to 2024. This is faster than the average rate of growth for all other occupations. This demand is directly connected to the population growth and the need for hair-care services. In addition, depending on the demographics of the population, the demand could be greater.

Essentially, this percentage increase indicates that there is a need for this occupation and needs spell opportunity. To capitalize on this opportunity, one must have a plan, be at the right place and location, and acquire the resources to make it happen. So, how do you start with a plan? It's simple because we all are equipped with an imagination. Whatever you imagine for your business, write it down on paper and type or speak it into your smart phone. This plan will be a very rough draft, and you will add to it, remix it and take away from it before you have a final plan. One important step is to develop a business plan. A business plan maps out how you're going to operate your business. If you need to finance your business, you must have a business plan. There are various organizations that can help you with your plan.

You will then seek out some level of assistance or wise counsel to determine if you can put your plan into action. If you already know how to put your plan in place, you have accomplished a great task. I caution you to be careful with whom you share your ideas. Share your ideas with only a few trusted people in your inner circle. After you have a solid plan, know what resources you need as well as startup costs for your barber shop. An important part of getting your plan in place is looking for the location for your barber shop. The location is very important for driving business and customers to your barber shop. This will be discussed in a later chapter.

Above-Average Median Income and Flexibility

Per the Bureau of Labor Statistics, barbers earn on average between \$17,940 and \$47,410 working full and/or part-time. Depending on the operation and vision of the barber, many barbers earn much more than the national averages. While those figures give you average salaries, I believe the amount you earn is dependent on your market (city), your strategy, brand and vision. However, the most important factor is that the barber makes and acts on the decision to take his business to greater heights. Some barbers are making thousands of dollars per cut with their superstar clientele!

Obtaining growth and wealth as a barber shop owner is determined by several factors. The vision of the barber shop owner is paramount. Like anything else we do without a vision, a business without a vision will fail and not capitalize on its true potential. Having a vision is the ability to see beyond what currently exists and knowing how to put the pieces together to make your dream a reality.

Knowing who your customers are is also important in the barbering business. Knowing your customers means understanding the age and social status of those you serve. When you can see that picture, you can customize your services around attracting and retaining that type of customer. What is of utmost importance in customer profiling is that you have your finger on the pulse of knowing your customers, because one wrong move could damage potential retention of your customers. Another determinant of your barbering business growth is its location.

You have probably heard that it is difficult to sell ice water outside at the South Pole. Well, it is difficult to operate a barber shop in an area that is not appealing to the customer's eyes and is uninviting.

Creating a diversity of products in your barbering business is also a determinant to the growth of your business. Today's barber shops offer a variety of services and products to produce and increase revenue. To offer various products and services requires the barber shop owner to develop relationships with vendors and to partner with individuals who specialize in areas that complement customers' needs.

Renting out space in your shop can be very profitable for your business. I see this as a two-fold opportunity. If the owner has a shop that is awesome and attracts customers throughout the community, that could attract a larger number of interested barbers. That interest, in turn,would give you the opportunity to select which barbers you want on your team. It is like having a dream team of barbers. By having your dream team, that attracts more customers, which brings more revenue.

Financial management is one of the most important factors in operating your business. You can make six figures, but if most of your money is going out the window toward various expenses and not investments to enhance the business, you are going down the wrong path. There are several software packages and counselors who can assist you with your business' financial operations, if you're not comfortable with that aspect of your business. However, I caution you to be thorough in selecting the right financial professional. Investigating requires asking for references and contacting them to check on their past performance. Contact the Better Business Bureau to see if there have been any complaints. This is worth your time because you don't want to put your business in a position where you are losing money.

Chapter 2 Questions

- What is your goal in becoming a barber?
- What are your financial goals?
- Where do you see yourself in 10 years?

Chapter 3: Turning My Barber Shop from a Hustle to a Legitimate Business

Cutting hair is something that many of us have the capability of doing, and some of us have cut hair in the past. I even took a stab at cutting hair while in the Marines. I would cut hair while in the barracks. Marines wanted a more stylish cut than just the regular high and tight, or what we'd call a soup bowl cut. It was called a soup bowl cut because your haircut looked like a bowl was placed on top of your head and all the hair was trimmed below the bowl. Nonetheless, I was not licensed to cut hair while in the Marines, and I received a statement from them asserting only authorized barbers could cut hair. If a Marine was caught cutting hair, he would be written up. That ended my quest for being a barber while in the military.

Several barbers have told me some barbers believe barbering is just a hustle, just to make extra money. This is puzzling because barbering is an excellent profession to expand and grow a business. Any profession you undertake, whether an accountant, plumber, or entertainer, the amount of time you put into your craft will determine your level of success. Success is not given; it is earned through hard work, commitment, and faith. That is my take, and I am sure many others have their view on it. I would even say barbering is a craft as well as an art because of all the different types of styles and designs available to customers. It is the process of being enlightened.

I don't believe people fall into situations for any random reason. I believe people are in situations, like being a barber, because that is their journey for that given time. What you do with it is totally dependent upon you. I was out with a person some years ago and he told me that many of our opportunities are right in front of our face, if only we'd open our eyes. That was profound to me because I do believe there are many opportunities in front of our face if we'd simply open our eyes. What I mean by opening our eyes is that while our eyes are physically open, we must determine if something is an opportunity or not. You can determine the pros and cons, and if your skillset is in alignment with the opportunity. What plagues us sometimes is that we have so much going on; we want that immediate gratification to make as much money as soon as possible. The reasons for that varies. It could be because of family obligations or the need and quest to be rich. But whatever the case may be, I do believe that we should take a step back and look at where we are, what we're doing, and where we're going.

In transforming your hustle into a legitimate business,

you first should start with looking into your inner self with how you see yourself and where you want to be. For whatever reason, we sometimes do not see opportunities that are right in front of our eyes, or we have our minds set on doing something that might not be in alignment with our talents. The best path for anyone to take is the path where your talents exist. Being a barber is a gift, and one must have talent to cut hair. Some are better than others. Quite honestly, I was only okay at barbering and would admit it was not my gift. Barbering also is an art, and to me, is like being an artist. You must have imagination and the skill to cut hair according to what the customer wants and cutting it so that it complements the customer.

Second, register your business with the federal, state, and local government. Your registration at the state level involves setting a business structure. There are many forms of business structures, but the most common forms of businesses in barbering are Sole Proprietorship, General Partnership, Corporations, and Limited Liability Company (LLC).

Sole Proprietorship

A sole proprietorship is a business that is owned by a single individual. It is the easiest type of business structure to form because no paperwork is needed to file with the state unless you want to run your business under a name different from your own. A license or permit and registration of business with your local government might be needed. This is attractive to many because their business would not be bogged down with government regulations. They also do not have to deal with oversight of partners, boards, or shareholders. Sole proprietors also can report their income on their personal taxes.

A major disadvantage of a sole proprietorship is that as the business owner, you are personally liable for any debt the business incurs. If sued, you are personally liable. That means all your assets (home, car, etc.) are vulnerable. In addition, it can be very difficult to get a bank loan as a sole proprietor.

Depending on your type of business, I would be a little hesitant to operate as a sole proprietor primarily because of the liability. I was at a conference, and this millionaire businessman said that once you start making money people will come after you and proposition you. I believe him. You want to protect your personal assets.

General Partnership

A general partnership is similar to a sole proprietorship; however, a general partnership involves two or more people. Therefore, a little more work must be done to divide up the business responsibilities and ownership percentages between both owners. Like the sole proprietorship, no paperwork needs to be filed with the state unless you want to operate under a different name.

The key drawback of a partnership is that you are personally liable for any of your partners' mistakes. If one of your partners accidentally injures a customer, both of you will be held liable, and that can affect your business and personal assets.

Having a partner can be a win-win situation for you both. I advise that each partner's role and every detail of the business be written in contractual form and notarized, because one never knows the future. Perhaps, a partner could get killed in an accident, leaving the other partner with uncomfortable decisions to make. I have worked with people who developed partnerships with their boyfriend and/or best friend, and that is good. I would just say that in business, it is easy for friendships to break down. Therefore, have a clear understanding of each other's management style and an understanding on the direction of the company.

Corporation

A corporation is a business entity that is recognized as a separate legal entity from its owners. A corporation is a whole different business structure. Corporations are more complicated to set up and understand than sole proprietorships and general partnerships. It has its ability to conduct business, sue, or be sued. There are several types of corporations, but the most common type for barbers is the S Corporation. Unlike the previous two business structures, there is actual paperwork required for an S Corporation.

An S Corporation, commonly called an S Corp, is a special corporation under the IRS tax code. Under this system, the profits and losses can pass through to your personal tax return and the business is not taxed. Only the owners of the business are taxed. This protects the corporation from double taxation. Corporations are taxed as a separate entity as well. There are tax savings benefits to this structure, but it does make business setup a bit more complicated.

The owners of a corporation are called shareholders. The primary advantage of having a corporation is the limited liability it grants its shareholders. What that means is an owner is only liable up to the amount he/she has invested in the business. Another benefit of a corporation is that it can implement a benefit and profit-sharing program for its employees.

Limited Liability Company (LLC)

The Limited Liability Company (LLC) is a business structure that acts as a corporation but is not one. It is not a corporation, but it can still provide the corporate-like protection that is important for many business owners. An LLC can be taxed as a sole proprietorship, partnership, or S Corp, and income and expenses can simply be passed through to the members'(owners) individual tax returns.

How you set up your barber shop will give you legitimacy to your barbering business and how you operate it could position you for greatness. It is extremely important to not mix your personal money with your business. How you treat your customers, your finances, and the activity in and around your business—and even the patrons of your barber shop—will tell the story about your business. Mainly, a (mis)perception held by some customers could negatively affect the shop. The marketing and the finances of your barber shop, not hustle, will be discussed in a later chapter.

Chapter 3 Questions

- **If you think your business is a hustle, what would it take for you to change your mindset?**
- **What is the best business structure for you?**
- **What perception do you want to give your customers?**

Chapter 4: From Legitimacy to Growth: Positioning Your Barber Shop to Grow

The beauty of owning your own business is that you are in total control of how it looks and where it's going. The pleasure to me in being a business owner is the ability to dream, and to put a vision in place that is going to help people. What I found is that often we come up with our vision from our experiences, both positive and negative, and we turn those experiences into power. When I say power, I'm saying it could be something that could change the face of the community or create a need for a customer base. So, in laying the foundation for your business, you must look at what direction you're going in and forecast where you see it in five, 10, 15, and 20 years. Some might look at this as a little crazy, because we don't know where we're going to be 20 years from now. However, we need to think ahead in everything we do regarding our life and business. For example, you might plan to own 20 different barber shops regionally 20 years from now. You also might plan to sell your barber shop to another company in 10 to 15 years. Those are legitimate plans a barber could put in place, and the sky is the limit with one's planning and investment for their business. So, in making this investment, how do we know if we are making a right business move? Are you selling just because of the dollar amount, or is the dollar amount offered at a fair market value for the investment? To safeguard our barbering business, we need to develop a business model to ensure that we get a fair Return on Investment (ROI).

A business model is how you're going to operate your barber shop: the direction it is going, what type of clientele you are to service, what type of services you're going to offer, and the list can go on and on. Your business model is taken from your experiences coupled with your know-how in running and operating a business. While owning and operating a business might be a new venture, I would advise that you seek wise counsel to assist you with developing your business model for your company. There are many services that can give you advice, both free and paid, regarding what resources are needed, what direction your company should go, and how it should be grown. I advise that once you get your business filed and make it legitimate, exercise wisdom with whom you do business and from whom you receive wise counsel. When your business is on fire with growth, you're going to have other companies that will solicit your business—claiming to be experts in their field, when in fact they are just another company looking to make money from you and give you a lot of false hopes and false dreams. Always do your research on a possible service provider as well as check references.

Many might think that a business model is the same as a business plan. It is not. A business plan outlines the operations of a company. A business model outlines how and what way your company will function. It plans out its day-to-day operations. A business model describes how the company's position within the industry value chain is and how it organizes its relations with potential customers. This will position your barber shop to maximize revenue as well as profit. So, how do you develop a business model for your barber shop?

For starters, look at what products and services you're going to offer while planning out your barber shop. I have been in hundreds of barber shops throughout the years. Many offer haircuts, and they might offer beverages as well as snacks. That is all fine and dandy, however, there are still other great opportunities for a barber to make money beyond cutting hair. So, when developing your vision for your barber shop, develop a list of what services and products you would like to offer in addition to cutting hair. For example, and in a traditional sense, a business model of services that the barber shop could provide include the following:

- **Haircuts for men and boys:** style, one-step hair color, highlights, toner, corrective color, hair and scalp treatments.

- **Natural haircuts for women:** Offering various styles and conditioning for maintaining and stimulating women's natural hair; one-step hair color, highlights, toner, corrective color.
- **Hair laser removal:** Hair removal on neck, back, ears, etc.
- **Scalp massage & conditioning treatment:** The massages often include heat and deep conditioning treatments that can relieve stress, induce relaxation.
- **Straight razor and wet shave:** Traditional straight-razor shaves, hot towels, and balm treatment
- **Beard sculpting:** Having the skillset of maintaining and grooming beards could be a difference maker in your business.
- **Gray blending and coloring:** This is very popular with men that are graying. Many might color their heads but partially gray their beards.
- **Facials:** Men and women both take advantage of this service.

Another business model service that I would say is non-traditional would be having a barber shop in a bar setting. This setup would offer beverages to the customers as they wait to get their haircut. This business model is currently in existence with Beards and Beer barber shop. I think this is a great and creative business model, and I am sure there are extra insurance liability costs as well because you have to be mindful of those that come into your shop to drink and need to drive home safely. Another business model that could be in a barber shop is having an expanded retail line of men's clothes and products. These clothes could range from sweatshirts, warmup suits, bow ties and much more. Types of products that could be offered would be various shaving creams, razors, and sports gear. When it comes to expanding a product line in a barber shop, the sky is the limit. I will say that with expanding and having a retail line, it is also important that you stay on top of your inventory so that you do not lose items. You can attach almost any product or service to the barber shop as it relates to your customers. You can attach a tax-service business to your barber shop, and your customers could get their taxes done while they wait for service. You can place a weight room as a form of recreation for your customers. Whatever the case, I would do my research and study what customers need in addition to haircuts. When you do that, you will be able to better determine what products and services you're going to put into your barber shop.

In conclusion, developing your business model for your barber shop will require time, effort and money. I would carefully think about what products or services to offer in addition to simply cutting hair. The prices of products and services could really be profitable for your barber shop if purchased at a good, reasonable price and sold to your customers. Develop a list of products and services you would like to provide; the cost of those products and services, and the price you're going to charge for those products and services. This would be a great starting point in planning your business model.

Chapter 4 Questions
- **How do you see your barber shop operating?**
- **What types of services would you like to offer your customers?**
- **What types of products would you like to offer your customers?**

Chapter 5: Having the Right Team in Your Barber Shop

In life, we all have been equipped with great imaginations and ideas. Some of us have the inherent instinct of leadership, while others have different abilities. We are equipped with great insight and vision. As we move our business forward to another level, we must have the right people and teams in place. Whether it's an employee in your company or a contract barber, having the right people and teams in place will either propel your business to greater heights or will sink your business into failure. So, in developing your barber shop and positioning it to go to a new level, having the right people and right teams in place is paramount. What do I mean by having the right people and the right teams in place?

Having the right people in place is very important in carrying out your expectations for operating an excellent business. Those expectations will provide excellent customer service to all customers. Another expectation is how you're going to present yourself to your customers, such as all team members dressed in uniforms with logos of the barber shop.

Your team might sport different haircuts to show your customers, as a form of promotion. Your team will also be responsible for maintaining barber shop rules and etiquette.

For example, no smoking or profanity while in the business.

You as the owner, must establish how you want your team members to look and how you want them to treat your customers. With that said, you cannot discriminate against any potential team members. Moreover, if they do not possess that skillset or meet the qualifications, they do not meet the standards of being on your team.

Finding the right person for your team, whether it is an employee or contract worker, requires an interview process. The interview does not have to be something formal, but it needs to happen. This interview process should consist of the potential team member filling out an application that lists his/her experiences as a barber. This will help you to determine their qualifications, skills, and abilities. During the interview, I would ask various questions about servicing customers, working in teams, handling different barbering situations, and handling conflict from unsatisfied customers. Below are sample questions to ask and not ask in an interview.

Questions to Ask a Potential Barber for your Business

- What motivated you to become a barber?
- Can you tell me more about yourself as a barber? What types of customers do you like working with and what types don't agree with you?

- What are your goals in becoming a barber?

- What is your ideal type of customer and barber shop?

- Tell me about a time you had a customer that did not like his/her haircut. What did you do to correct this issue? Walk me through the process.

- Where do you see yourself in ten years?

- What attracted you to apply to work at XYZ barber shop?

- Tell me about the professional relationships you have developed at work. How would you describe the best ones? The worst? Did they help your barbering career?

- How do you distinguish between hard work and smart work?

- What is something you could do every day for the rest of your career?

Questions to Not Ask a Potential Barber for Your Business

- Are you married?
- What is your race and gender?
- What country were you born in?
- How old are you?
- What is your religion?
- Are you disabled?

Be mindful that when you are asking questions you are

not discriminating no matter how comfortable you become with the interviewee. If you are not comfortable with developing questions or knowing what types of questions to ask, consult with a Human Resources professional. Another form of ensuring you have the right person on your team is to have all potential team members tested to determine their skillsets. You can set up a mock situation and have them cut different styles to determine their skill level and versatility. This might sound cumbersome, but there is nothing more costly than hiring the wrong persons and having to figure out ways to remove them from your team.

While you might have great expectations of having people on your team, you must have respect for them and have an open line of communication. While communicating, you must be transparent, honest, and open to feedback. One sure way to get someone on your team is to listen to and value their feedback. I know this will be hard for some to do but, being the owner, acknowledging and complimenting them can go a long way.

As an incentive to get the right people on your team, determine what benefits you can offer team members and what it takes to attract the best team players. For instance, in addition to your chair rental, you also could offer profit sharing and business investment initiatives to build more commitment from your team members and to drive business. You also could offer a 401K plan for retirement and, based on their number of years of service, you could contribute a percentage. As a note, speak with a financial advisor on the different options you could offer your team members. If you are not at the position to financially support your team, you can always provide mentoring. Mentoring consists of providing guidance and instruction within a profession, and in life. This could be powerful because it strengthens trust and understanding between you and the team member.

Finally, it is important that you establish the right set of rules and expectations as well as set up ways where you can recruit and hire the right team players that believe in and embrace your vision. You should weigh what you can offer to incentivize your team members and determine what you can pay and invest to strengthen your empire.

Chapter 5 Questions
- **What type of barber will be on your team?**
- **What can you initially offer your barbers?**

Chapter 6: Managing Your Numbers: Barber Shop Financial Management

Running and operating any business requires sound financial management. If you do not operate it properly, the business most likely will fail. That is the reality. The beauty of running a barber shop is that it is somewhat recession-proof. What I mean by recession-proof is this: Regardless of the economy, people still need their hair cut, because they want to look nice. When the economy is not good some will look at other alternatives, but many people will continue to go to barber shops to get a haircut as well as to chat with the fellas.

Managing Your Cash

Managing your cash is extremely important to your livelihood and growth of your barber shop. Given that barbering is still a cash-based business, it is easy to lose track of your finances if you do not have a system of deposits in place. For example, if you make $500 a day in cash payments, what do you do with your money? Do you deposit it in the bank, keep the money on you, or take it home to store it? If you are depositing the money in the bank, you are on the right track. What is key is the frequency of your deposits, but I advise you to deposit your money at least, every two days. If you could do it every day, that would be even better. Depositing your money in the bank not only secures your money, it also shows a record of the money you are earning, and you could use that as a means of acquiring personal or business loans. I have spoken to many people who believe keeping money on you helps to secure you. That is wrong. Keeping money on you puts you at risk for losing/misplacing the money or, even worse, getting robbed. Even if you store your money in your home, what if a disaster occurs, such as a tornado or a fire? You stand the chance of literally losing it all. By implementing a system for depositing your cash, that puts you in a better financial position.

Financial Management of Your Business

Knowing the financial position of your barber shop is not rocket science. It is a matter of knowing where your money is coming from and where it is going. I am going to go over tips and practices to show how you should look at operating the financial aspect of your business. As a businessperson, experience proves that it is extremely important for you to know the basics of financial management. Leaving your financial matters in the hands of others is not only unacceptable, but also a recipe for failure. I am not saying you should not rely on wise counsel. I am saying your counsel should have integrity and credibility, and measures must be put in place to safeguard your earnings. For example, every dollar and cent that is transacted should be accounted for. If you are writing checks and you are the owner, only you should sign the checks.

What I am going to cover next are some basic accounting terms and strategies so you can see the profitability of your business. Various software systems are available that can assist you in understanding and painting a picture of your barber shop's financial position. I would advise that you purchase software such as Intuit QuickBooks or Tax Matters. In addition, seek the advice of a Certified Public Accountant (CPA).

Some basic financial statements you should distinguish are income statements and cash-flow statements. The income statement shows the profit and loss of your barber shop. When you cut hair, the sales from cutting hair are called income or "revenue." The supplies, equipment, chair rental, and utilities paid are classified as "expenses." For example, if you make $7,000 cutting hair during a period of time and your expense were $4,300, you would profit (net profit) $2,700 (See example):

Income Statement of XYZ Barber Shop
for the period ending September 30, 2022

INCOME

Services Rendered $7,000.00

Total Income   **$7,000.00**

EXPENSES

Property Lease $1,500.00
Telephone and Internet $300.00
Water and Electricity $500.00
Insurance $300.00
Advertising Cost $500.00
Taxes $1,000.00
Bank Charges $200.00

Total Expenses   **$4,300.00**

NET PROFIT (Total Income - Total Expenses)   **$2,700.00**

On the other hand, if you make $7,000 cutting hair during a period of time and your expenses were $8,200, your **loss** during that time would be $1,200.

Income Statement of XYZ Barber Shop
for the period ending September 30, 2022

INCOME

Services Rendered	$6,000.00
Chair Rental	$1,000.00
Total Income	**$7,000.00**

EXPENSES

Property Lease	$4,000.00
Telephone and Internet	$300.00
Water and Electricity	$500.00
Insurance	$500.00
Advertising Cost	$500.00
Taxes	$2,000.00
Bank Charges	$400.00
Total Expenses	**$8,200.00**

NET PROFIT (Total Income - Total Expenses)	($1,200.00)

As you see, the income statement will show the different categories and how your expenses will fluctuate or remain the same over time.

For example, a mortgage or lease payment will remain the same for that **period of time,** unless you have an adjustable mortgage rate, or you are renewing your lease. Examples of variable expenses (expenses that changes based on the amount of usage) would be your utilities and advertising costs. Now we know that if you continuously take a loss, you will be out of business soon.

According to *Inc. Magazine,* a cash flow statement is a financial report that describes where revenue is generated at a specific period of time. This statement is useful in determining how functional a company is in the short-term, particularly its ability to pay bills (see example below). The management of your cash flow is very important for your barber shop because it will give you a picture of the amount of cash on hand and if you can expand or invest more in your business.

Cash Flow Statement of XYZ Barber Shop
for the period ending September 20, 2022

Cash receipts from customers	$7,000.00
Cash paid to suppliers	-$2,000.00
Cash generated from operations	$5,000.00
CASH FLOW FROM OPERATING ACTIVITIES	$5,000.00
CASH FLOW FROM INVESTING ACTIVITIES	
Addition to equipment	-$4,000.00
Net cash flow from investing activities	-$4,000.00
CASH FLOW FROM FINANCING ACTIVITIES	
Proceeds from loan	$5,000.00
Payment to loan	-$500.00
Net cash flow from financing activities	$4,500.00
NET INCREASE/DECREASE IN CASH	$5,500.00
Cash at the beginning of the period	
Cash at the end of the period	$5,500.00

The difference between the income and cash-flow statement is income statements consider some of the non-cash accounting items, such as depreciation. The cash-flow statement omits that and shows exactly how much actual money the business has generated. Cash-flow statements show how the business has performed in managing inflows and outflows of cash. It also provides a sharper picture of a company's ability to pay creditors and finance growth.

Paying Your Taxes

The barber shop business is primarily a cash business, meaning barbers accept payment in the form of cash. Many barbers have evolved to accept payment through credit cards, Cashapp, and Zelle. With accepting payment through cash, you would have a lot of discretion in how you report your earnings. I have been told that some report accurate amounts and others do not. Whether you are reporting the accurate amount or not, I state below why you should report it accurately.

For starters, paying taxes is the law. There is no way to get around it. There are ways in which you do not have to pay as much, and I advise you seek out a Certified Public Accountant (CPA) to stay abreast of tax laws and to exercise the benefit of being a business owner. Secondly, big brother, that is, the IRS, always figures out a way to catch up with you. I once facilitated a community event on entrepreneurship and one of the speakers was from the IRS. At the end of the presentation, the presenter said we know who you are, meaning, we know who is doing what. Now, I am not trying to scare you and I don't believe that the IRS knows every single person failing to not report revenues accurately. What I do believe is sometimes people might cheat a little without getting caught. By not getting caught, they continue, and their cheating grows over time. As the cheating continues, it becomes more noticeable. For example, when one reports that they make $40,000 annually and they are living in a $300,000 home, driving a 7 series BMW, when in fact they are making $90,000. That brings attention to yourself from friends and the IRS. Sadly, there could come a time when you might get audited and be ordered to pay back taxes, penalties, or even worse, serve time in jail.

The Effects of Not Paying Taxes or Not Having Proper Documentation

Not reporting or paying taxes also affected individuals and businesses during the 2020 pandemic. The Small Business Administration (SBA) made available monies for independent contractors and businesses to receive grant funding and loans to sustain their businesses. During the first round, the SBA took the word of applicants and disbursed funds according to what applicants submitted on their applications. The SBA discovered widespread fraud. In the second round, the SBA required independent contractors and small businesses to submit their taxes to verify requested amounts matched tax documents. This closed the door for a lot of individuals and businesses to receiving the much-needed support from the SBA. Many businesses closed due to not having the proper documents or not knowing how to navigate through the application process.

Outside of being required to pay taxes because it is the law, paying taxes ensures social security for you. This is accomplished by paying your self-employment taxes. The self-employment tax is paid to the federal government to fund Medicare and Social Security. Medicare is the federal health insurance program for people who are 65 or older, certain younger people with disabilities, and people with End-Stage Renal Disease (www.medicare.gov). When you pay into the Social Security system, Social Security benefits are paid out monthly to retired workers. You typically pay 15.3 percent in self-employment taxes. However, you may claim a deduction for a portion on your tax return. You must report your earnings and when you pay your annual taxes. You will be paying your Social Security taxes based on the profits of your business. By doing so, you are setting up to receive some form of compensation when you retire. I once spoke to a barber just starting as a business owner, and he told me that he noticed a lot of older men were still barbering. That was because they did not pay their taxes accordingly, so they had to continue to work to generate income.

I see that as a stressful situation because I believe as you reach retirement age, work should be a choice, not a must.

Investing In Yourself and Future

In today's economy, receiving just a Social Security check may not fully cover one's standard of living. There are options you could invest into lowering your tax liability (taxes you pay). One such option is an Individual Retirement Account (IRA). An IRA is a type of savings account that is designed to help you save for retirement, and it offers many tax advantages. There are several types of IRAs: Traditional IRAs, Roth IRAs, SIMPLE IRAs and SEP IRAs. Individual Retirement Accounts (IRA) consist of a range of financial products such as stocks, bonds or mutual funds (www.investopedia.com). A Solo 401(k), (also known as a Self Employed 401(k) or Individual 401(k)), is a 401(k) qualified retirement plan for Americans. It is designed specifically for employers with no full-time employees other than the business owner and their spouse (money.cnn.com).

There are other forms of investments one could invest in even before retirement. One could invest in real estate and the stock market. Investing in real estate or the stock market are excellent ways of creating wealth. When invested in properly, one could speed up achieving their financial goals. However, investing is a discipline and a lifetime process. Whatever you decide to do, please seek wise counsel by speaking to a financial professional, and in seeking it, do your research.

Chapter 6 Questions

- Who will manage your day-to-day transactions?
- Do you need a financial professional to assist you with your finances?
- What are your financial business goals?
- Have you set up a system for paying your taxes?
- Have you ever invested or are planning to invest?

Chapter 7: Strategies for Marketing and Branding Your Barber Shop

When you see golden arches, what do you think of? McDonalds? When you see the red bullseye, what comes to mind? Target? There are many more images that we immediately think of because those organizations have strong brands. These strong brands would not be possible without the strategic marketing efforts that promote the organization through various marketing channels. All businesses must market their products and services, and if you want your barber shop business to grow, you must develop a plan to reach new and existing customers. In this section I will discuss what marketing and branding are and how they can both help your barber shop business thrive.

What Is Marketing?

Marketing is defined as the "strategic activities to promote, attract, and sell a product or service." Marketing operates on four spheres, called the 4Ps of marketing. The 4Ps are Product, Price, Place, and Promotion. The goal of marketing is to convert marketing strategies into sales through telling a story and getting a message across to those that want or need that product or service. That message comes in various forms: through social media, television, billboards, the newspaper, magazines, snail mail, and email. The message is also targeted for those that need to see it.

So, as a barber shop owner, how do you market your product and services and build a brand? You must develop a strategy that includes referrals, advertising, promotions, and endorsements. Even the simple task of sending an email or returning customer calls can be considered as marketing efforts.

How Do You Market Your Barber Shop?

Successfully marketing your barber shop will help in positioning your business to be profitable. Marketing coupled with quality service will convert customers into repeat customers. And if your service is great, you will have customers come from the surrounding neighborhoods, because word will travel. So, how does one market his barber shop to attract customers? While there are thousands of barber shops around, how does one make his barber shop unique? The answer is looking at what your competitors are doing, determining what your customers need, and adding a twist to what your barber shop offers. When you combine those factors, you will be on your way to applying the 4Ps to your marketing strategy.

Product

As a barber you are selling your service, which is hair cutting. In terms of marketing, you should look at your service as a product. You should view it in terms of how you are going to present and sell it to the customer. With any product, how it is presented (its packaging) is what catches the attention of the buyer. As a business teacher, I have taught many courses in how presentation is key. I have emphasized that any product or service needs to be presented on top of a China plate and not a garbage can lid. What I mean by that is that you want your product or service to be appealing to the eye. To appeal to the eye as a barber, you need to show examples of your work. Now I have been to countless barber shops where I have seen the poster with models on it and you tell the barber the style number you want. But if you want to set yourself apart from the rest, why not create your own personal board of some of your own creative work? You could even display additional original hairstyles. Creating your own hairstyle board would add to your presentation of work. It is also possible for you to offer haircare products to your clientele.

Price

Price refers to the amount that you will charge your customers for the services the barber shop provides. Your pricing strategy will play a crucial role in your marketing plan. You cannot simply grab a number from the air and publish it. There are numerous factors to consider when pinning down your pricing strategy. It comes down to two things. The first is your cost and profit margin. You should make sure that your price will help you generate enough profit to make the business grow. The second consideration is your pricing scheme. It must be competitive, not too low and not too high. You need to research a benchmark among similar businesses in your area. Conduct a competitor price check to see how your pricing strategy will fare in the local market. Do not be too quick to make your prices lower than your competition. Sometimes, it can make the business look cheap and, in effect, turn off potential customers. If you have excellent service and offer something that your competitors do not, then a higher pricing model could be ideal. Find the middle ground and adjust as you add or take away services.

Place

Place refers to the location of your barber shop. As you put together your marketing plan, the location of your business will play an important role in determining the foot traffic of your barber shop. The place where you will position your barber shop should be convenient for your target market. For instance, if you are targeting military personnel, then your business should be located near a military base. If your target customers are college students, then it should be near a college or university.

Promotion

Promotion refers to the specific marketing steps that you will take to tell your targeted customer about your product, price and place. You have many options. You can put out an ad in the local paper, attend trade shows, or you can hand out flyers. You also can visit radio stations in your area and ask them to promote your barber shop. Use social media sites. Make sure you know where your target market usually hangs out. You need to get your promotion prominent in places they frequent. The above-mentioned advertisement strategies cost money. There is nothing like the power of marketing your business through community service and networking. The phenomenal thing about both serving others and letting people know what you are doing, plant the seeds that will assist your business in attracting customers. Once you attract those customers, it is up to you to water that seed so your business will continue to grow.

Cost-Effective Ways to Market Your Barber Shop?

All marketing efforts will cost you something, whether it be money or your time. You should be prepared for both if you want to let your target customer know about your barber shop. Fortunately, promoting your business does not have to be expensive.

One of the good things about a barber shop is that you can only cater to the local market because it is very rare that a customer will drive a long way to get a haircut. Usually, they only look within their local area to find a barber shop. Therefore, your marketing reach does not have to be too far, which will cost you less.

There are various ways for you to make your marketing efforts cost-efficient. It all begins with a deeper knowledge of your target market. Again, you need to know where they hang and the places they frequent so you can concentrate your marketing efforts there. There is no use in promoting your business in places no one goes. So, what exactly can you do to promote your business in the most cost-efficient way? Here are some of your options:

- Look to establish partnerships with local businesses. For instance, you can give out special discounts to patrons of a particular store as long as they will allow you to post a sign to advertise in their store and vice versa.

- Use social media. This is one of the cheapest and most effective ways to market your barber shop without spending too much. You simply should create a Facebook page and invite people to your site. Post activities, promotions, discounts, and events of the barber shop. You can include before and after photos of your customers so potential customers will know what people in your barber shop can do. Be sure to get the consent of your customers before posting their pictures on social media.

- Find local publications and get permission to insert a two-for-one haircut coupon. This could also be placed on your social media pages. This should entice potential customers to visit the barber shop to avail themselves of your services. You can price it a little higher than the usual haircut, and the second one will be free.

- Be a part of local events. Check the community listings and determine if you can participate in upcoming events by conducting low-price haircuts in the venue. The local community will advertise these events and you can expect heavy foot traffic. You can take advantage of that exposure. Feel free to hand out flyers of your price list during the event as well as do Facebook live postings to promote and speak with customers.

These are only a few of the things that you can do to market your barber shop without spending too much. Partnering with other businesses, being on social media, and being community oriented, helps to establish and solidify your brand.

What Is Branding?

One key ingredient in your marketing efforts is branding. Your brand means that when people see your logo, they recognize your business. When they hear your business' name, they think of your product and services, and when they think of your business, they either want to go to it or stay away from it. Branding is where you communicate your message to your target market. As the owner of your barber shop, how you and team members carry themselves is a part of your business' brand.

Below are questions you need to consider. Answering the questions will assist you in recognizing and establishing your brand.

- How do you see yourself?
- What do you offer that is unique?
- How does your business look on the outside and inside?
- What sets you apart from other barber shops?
- How do customers view you?
- What does your customer expect from your business?

These are some of the key questions you need to address while developing your brand.

How Do You Brand Your Barber Shop?

I have been to various barber shops and have experienced many different settings—good, bad, and ugly. I have been in the peaceful barber shops where customers stay to themselves. I have been in those where the men discussed church, politics, and the community. And I have been in some where I walked in, then out, because it appeared I needed to put on a bulletproof vest. In all those cases, those experiences have stayed with me, whether good or bad. So, as a barber shop owner, what experience do you want your customers to remember? It starts with branding.

Let us begin with the logo. Your business logo serves as that single image that encompasses your whole business. We all know the symbolic image of the red, white, and blue barbering pole. In addition to the pole, you need to create a logo that will capture the essence of your services to customers. It also should embody the personality and character of your business. This then serves as the main anchor by which you evoke a certain mindset from people, depending on how good your services are. If customers leave your barber shop highly satisfied, they will equate it to your business, and ultimately, identify your business by your logo. This is one of those psychological phenomena with images; if service was great, what we see will serve as a reminder. This underscores the importance of the quality service you provide. This also increases the chances of developing brand champions. On their own, customers will tell their network of family and friends about the wonderful experience they received. They become part of your organic marketing mix.

Another element of your brand is the "curb appeal." This simply means that potential customers are enticed to physically drop in your shop because of how it looks from the outside. This can be as simple as clean windows and neon signs or even a nice decor out front. This helps drive foot traffic into your barber shop, and helps customers associate your brand with a specific appeal.

Since a barber shop is mostly geared toward men, it is a good idea to think of adjacent products that would cater to your market. Most men might want to have a drink while waiting for their turn. It can be anything from water to soda and even hard drinks. If you are in a family-oriented location, allocating a small space where kids can play or watch their shows could go a long way. Offering free Wi-Fi may also create extra business. These extra services then become part of your appeal that could entice people to walk through the door.

You also can incorporate convenience with your marketing efforts for your brand. Are you located in a fast-paced environment? If so, then you can include the availability of being able to schedule a haircut at specific times in a day. If there is a big population of older people, home service would also be a great idea, but please check with licensing in your area.

Regardless of how you market or brand your barber shop, it is important to remember that you need to stay true to the identity of your business model and your target market. It will do you good to promote the business in a way that is most appealing to your target market. In summary, you will not gain customers if you fail to look appealing to your target customer, so you need to continually find ways to determine your target market's needs and appeal to them.

Chapter 7 Questions

- How do you plan to market your business?

- How do you plan to brand your business?

- How does your customer look (age, race, profession, etc.)?

Chapter 8: Am I My Customer's Keeper? Customer Service and Loyalty Strategies

Your customers play an important part in the success of your business. This is the reason why you need to consider yourself as your customer's keeper. You want to make sure they are satisfied with your service because they will be the ones to bring in the money that keeps your barber shop thriving. Let me stress: Without customers, you will not have a successful business.

In this section, I will discuss customer service, specifically how you can provide it with excellence. It is extremely important to offer great customer service, even if you are having a bad day or a customer is a jerk. You should be mindful you have people watching you, and overreacting could damage your reputation and business.

What Is Customer Service?

Did you know that 45 percent of customers are willing to pay more if you provide better customer service? This is according to the recent survey done by Accenture about customer engagement. In fact, there is an estimate of $1.6

trillion worth of business that is lost due to poor customer service. In the barbering business, customer service and timing are extremely important. If you want to maintain and attract more customers, offer high quality with timely cuts, and you will have repeat customers.

What Exactly Is This Type of Service?

Customer service is the support that you offer your customers both before, during, and after they receive a product or service. It refers to the effort you place on taking care of the needs of the customers that patronize your business. It is the protocol that you follow to provide and deliver high-quality, professional, and efficient products and services. The goal in providing customer service is to ensure that customers have a great experience while transacting business with your company—in this case, your barber shop.

Some businesses lose customers because they only focus on the before and during phases, or they simply don't know how to offer customer service. The killer to me is when business owners are rude in offering customer service. They come off like they are doing you a favor by **allowing** you to purchase their product or service. Go figure! Even more, they fail to put an effort in providing customer support after the customer has paid them. And don't try to return the item! If you do right **by your** customers, your effort will eventually help you gain loyal ones. You will turn new customers into loyal customers. This helps you take your business to the next level.

Why Is Customer Service Important to Your Barber Shop?

There are two words that sum up the importance of customer service to your barber shop: branding and reputation.

Branding and Reputation

Your business is service-oriented. You are selling your ability to meet the needs of your customers. You need to make sure you do a good job at it, and that your customers will have a wonderful experience while visiting your barber shop. This is how you can build a strong brand and reputation not just with your target market, but also with your competitors.

So How Does Customer Service Help with Building the Brand of Your Barber Shop?

The brand of a company is what comes to mind when customers hear of your barber shop. It is the expectation that your customers have toward your business. When they see the name or logo of your barber shop, in their minds they form expectations.

The thing is, these expectations are often formed by the experience they have every time they interact with your company. Every positive interaction you have with your customer results in a favorable branding message. Of course, every interaction is defined by how well your customer service efforts are laid out. If you have bad customer service skills, that is the branding message that you will relay to your customers.

When you keep sending a negative branding message, you can bet it will build into a bad reputation for your barber shop. In today's digital age, having a bad reputation can quickly spread like wildfire. People will share just about anything online, specifically the bad experiences. If you do not pay attention to the customer service in your barber shop, that can be the end of your business. Sometimes all it takes is one bad experience, a well-crafted post and some shares to ruin your reputation. When that happens, you can say goodbye to new customers. It may or may not do anything to your loyal customers, but it could damage your earning potential.

As you can see, your service or prices will play an important role in attracting customers into your barber shop. However, it is the experience that will ultimately help convert your guests into loyal customers.

What Happens If You Provide Poor Customer Service?

If you fail to pay attention to your customer service and it ends up giving your customers a bad experience, there are a couple of things that will happen.

- *Negative word-of-mouth marketing occurs.* First, you can say goodbye to one of the most effective marketing arms that you will have. Word-of-mouth marketing is the free advertisement that you can get from previous customers. If they have a bad experience, they will be sure to tell people they know. As mentioned, the digital age has made it easy for people to share their experiences. Word will quickly spread that your barber shop fails at customer service.

- *Loss of new customers.* The negative publicity will surely compromise your ability to get new customers. Usually, new customers will look at reviews about a company before they try out a product or service. If your barber shop receives negative reviews, potential customers will hesitate before they use your haircutting services.

- **Damage to existing customer base.** Not only will you compromise the ability to get new customers, you also will damage confidence with existing customers. They may continue to use your services for now. But if they experience the bad customer service or if a new barber shop opens with a better reputation, it is possible for you to lose these customers as well.

- **Decrease in profit.** Once you start losing customers, your revenue will be affected next. Obviously, your customers pay you for your services. If they stop coming, you will lose that source of revenue. The bad customer service can seriously compromise your earning potential.

Obviously, when your revenues start to go down, it can only go from bad to worse. The employee morale also will go down. Not only that, but the stability of the business also suffers. If you do not act fast and improve your customer service, you might see yourself closing your barber shop.

Fortunately, bad customer service should not be the end of it all for your business. You can still salvage it if you act quickly. People make mistakes, and sometimes that results in a bad customer experience. So, what can you do if you have an incident of bad customer service?

Start by coming up with a resolution with the affected customers. Reach out and talk to them. Try not to be too defensive, especially when you know that it is the barber shop and your employees that were at fault. What you want to do is appease the customers before they spread the word about their negative experience. There are times when a bad experience can land you a loyal customer, but only if you know how to treat the customer and the issue correctly.

There are many ways you can do this. You can issue a refund. Or you can give a coupon or a free haircut the next time they visit. You need to give them a reason to come back so you can redeem yourself.

After resolving the issues with the customer, the next step is to investigate what went wrong. Sometimes, a bad action is all there is to it. However,there are times when the bad action is a result of poor customer service skills or defective management. Try to get to the root cause of the customer service problem so it will never happen again.

If bad publicity has already spread, you may want to issue an official statement to explain what happened. It is not a guarantee that everyone will believe you, but it might convince some to give you a chance.

Different Types of Customer Services and Strategies to Create Loyalty

There are many ways to implement good customer service in your barber shop. To identify what will work best, you need to first get to know who your customers are. The key to making this successful is to keep in mind you need to put the customer first. Here are a few tips you can use for your barber shop:

- *Come up with a unique greeting.* This is something that your employees will say whenever someone enters the barber shop. You can choose to have them shout it in unison or just have the receptionist say it. This greeting should reflect the branding of your barber shop.

- *Give a genuine compliment.* Your barber shop is there to make your customers look physically good. Your employees should learn how to deliver a sincere compliment because you want the customers to feel good about themselves. Go the extra mile with haircare suggestions and reminders. You want the customers to feel as if you care about them. They do not only want to be appreciated, they also want to know that you sincerely want them to look good. Your employees should give suggestions and reminders on proper haircare.

- **Offer something before the customer leaves.** This can be a product or a loyalty card that offers perks and discounts. Train your employees how to offer these without sounding like a salesperson.

- **Thank customers for coming to your barber shop.** What the customers hear before they leave will stick with them. In addition to thanking them, wish them a good day and encourage them to come back. Be sure to show them your appreciation for visiting the barber shop.

These are general ways that you can make your customers feel good while they are in your barber shop. Remember, you want them to have the best experience while they are with you. It is your chance to prove why they need to return to your shop to avail themselves of more services.

Developing a List of Customers

A list of customers or a customer list is simply a database that holds the information of your customers. There are reasons why you need this list. First, this list will allow you to connect with your customers so you can give them more information about your services. In case there are new promos or discounts, this list will help you inform your customers. It is a great way to give your customer base a nudge so they will help you earn more profit. Also, a customer list will allow you to generate feedback and surveys that will help you improve your customer service and overall product/service offers.

Now that you know why your barber shop needs a customer list, the next question that we need to discuss is how you can generate that list. Here are a couple of options:

Have a guestbook ready. Every customer that walks into your barber shop should be encouraged to write required information in this book. You could use a booklet and/or an electronic device to collect customer information.

Develop a website. This website will provide potential customers with the services and products that your barber shop offers. It should also have a "Contact Us" page where the website visitor can get in touch with your company. Make sure you give the site visitors all the opportunities to input their details (e.g., pop-ups, opt-in).

Create a social media page. This is proving to be one of the most effective ways to keep your target market aware of your activities. A Facebook, Instagram, TikTok, and Twitter account will help you connect with your customer base. Through this portal, you can view potential customers and send them private messages to encourage them to visit your barber shop.

Check local business listings. This is a classic way of getting a customer list. There are companies that sell consumer contact details. This will give you a cold list of customers that you can call or send a message to so they will know your barber shop exists.

Look at the local paper or Yellow Book. This is another classic way of calling in customers. Since your target market is probably in the neighborhood, make sure to concentrate on a local listing.

Once you have a list, make sure you start to actively connect with your customers. This will encourage them to come and visit you at the barber shop.

Direct Mail and Email Marketing Campaigns

The best and probably most cost-efficient way to connect with your customer list is through direct mail and email marketing campaigns. According to an article published on HBR.org, an email marketing campaign will help you know within 24 hours which recipients have opened your mail. When it comes to direct mail, a study reveals that it has the higher response rate compared to an email marketing campaign, but it costs a bit more to do. Before you decide how to use them both, let us explore each option.

Direct Mail Marketing

Direct mail marketing means "snail mail." You will print out your campaigns, promotions, and discounts, place them in an envelope with the details of the promotion or offer, and mail it the traditional way. The reception will take longer. However, the chances of the mail being viewed by the recipient are higher.

The downside to this is that the process will be more time-consuming and more expensive. The key to doing a direct mail marketing campaign is follow-up with the mail recipient.

Email Marketing

Email marketing is the least expensive way to roll out a campaign. It is also the easiest to deliver. You can draft one email and send it to hundreds or even thousands of customers with just one click. It is also easiest to track. There are systems and programs that will help you identify which of the recipients have opened your email. Probably a downside to this is that your email campaign will most likely be buried under the many emails that the recipient receives every day. It might even be included in their spam folder. This makes the reception less favorable compared to direct mail.

Instead of choosing between the two, it might be a good idea to use both. Without a doubt, these two should be a part of your marketing campaigns, because it will also be a reflection of your customer service efforts.

Chapter 8 Questions

- **What are you going to do to handle customer conflicts?**
- **Who are your best customers?**

Chapter 9: My Barber Shop Is My Castle: Strategies on Location, Curb Appeal, and Shop Maintenance

In some reality shows, we see beautiful homes and cars of stars, whose plush life would inspire anyone to dream. You cannot help but be attracted to them, wanting to go inside or live in them, right? It would cause anyone to dream.

In this section I will discuss how the right curb appeal will help you attract customers. We will use what you have learned about marketing and branding to come up with an overall strategy to maintain and grow your barber shop.

Why Is Location Important to Driving Business?

Location is important to businesses that sell products or provide services directly to their customers because it plays a vital role in driving customers into your business. If you are in a high-traffic area, that increases your chances for new and walk-in customers. Walk-in customers are vital to the success of a barber shop. The more upscale or prominent barber shops require appointments, but if you are just starting out, you need these walk-in customers to get you through each day. This is one of the main reasons why you need to choose a location that will give your barber shop two important things: high visibility and accessibility.

High Visibility

First, the barber shop must be highly visible. People should be able to see it as they pass by. As much as possible, you want to choose a place that has high foot traffic. Commercial businesses close to neighborhoods are a great place to start, but these are usually expensive to rent. Not only that, the competition also will be fierce, both in intensity and in space.

Accessibility

The location that you will choose should also be easily accessible. Take extra care to find a place that is accessible, on a public transportation route, and absolutely to people with disabilities. Ideally, you want your barber shop on the lower floor. If that is not possible, make sure the stairs or elevator can easily be used and will not hinder customers from accessing your business.

These two suggestions will help you get as many walk-in customers as possible. Apart from these two, you should also remember that the location of your business should take into consideration your target market. For instance, if you want to cater to families, setting up your barber shop in a mall would be a great idea. If your target market is students, as earlier stated, you want to stay near college campuses or universities. The location of your barber shop also will play a role in defining the image and brand that you want your business to project.

Cleanliness Is a Virtue: Benefits of a Clean Barber Shop

Once you have selected the right location for your barber shop, you also should consider how you will set up the business. We are not yet going to talk about the layout. We want to start with the cleanliness of your barber shop.

Let's face it, a barber shop can get very dirty quite fast. You cut hair, after all. It gets everywhere. Not only that, but the other services you also offer will make a mess. You want to make sure you can keep your barber shop clean. The way you present your barber shop speaks volumes about the service you offer. If you cannot maintain cleanliness in your shop, then how can the customers trust you to make their hair look good? It really pays to have someone in your shop to make sure that the shop is consistently clean, including prioritizing cleaning the floors and rest rooms. Most importantly, from a health and safety perspective, you want to make sure all areas of your barber shop are sanitized.

Sanitation of the tools is mandatory. Are your scissors, blades, and other tools clean? No customers would want to have your tools touch them if the tools are not cleaned properly. You do not have to make a show of cleaning your tools in front of your customers, but make sure they look presentable. You should make sure the cleanliness in your barber shop adheres to health and safety standards.

Apart from the overall cleanliness and sanitation, make sure your barber shop is also organized and in order. A well-kept shop speaks volumes about the owner and those working in it. The way you arrange your tools and hair products can help add to the overall ambiance of the shop.

Strategies for Maintaining an Attractive Place for the Customer

When you are decorating your barber shop, there are two things that you need to consider: your customers and your services. Since your customers are mostly men, you need to think about what is appealing and attractive to them. You should choose the right colors that will make them want to come back to your shop. For instance, grays, blue, and earth tones may be more appropriate compared to bright colors and feminine shades like pink and lavender.

Thinking about your customers will help you choose the

right equipment and appliances. For instance, a soft high-back chair is a great choice since your customers can relax while enjoying a haircut. If you cater to children, you should have one chair small enough for them, or a highchair. Some barber shops are really upscale. Some of you might remember the man who set the tone of eloquence in barber shops, Alonzo Herndon. Called the Crystal Palace, Herndon opened his barber shop in 1913 on Atlanta's Peachtree Street. It featured mahogany and plate glass doors to a long, elegant parlor lined with French beveled mirrors lit by crystal chandeliers and wall lamps. The room accommodated 25 custom barber chairs that were outfitted with porcelain, brass, and nickel, upholstered in dark-green Spanish leather (*Alonzo and His Crystal Palace*, August 2011). Mr. Herndon knew what he wanted and carried out his vision.

While you might not decide to have chandeliers, you should have your shop decorated in such a way that it is appealing and allows you to perform services efficiently. You want enough space to move around. As your barber shop grows, you will probably add more services. Make sure there is room for upgrades in your shop.

One area you need to pay special attention to is the waiting area. When you start getting more customers, or if they come all at the same time, you want to make sure they are comfortable while they wait. Otherwise, they might get up and leave to avail themselves of the services of another shop. Choose comfortable chairs and provide entertainment to keep them occupied while waiting in line.

Chapter 9 Questions

- **List areas that need to be cleaned. How often is this done?**
- **Whose responsibility is it to keep the barber shop clean?**

Chapter 10: Using Technology to Operate Your Business and to Reach and Grow Your Customer Base

Technology is aggressively taking over every phase of our society. If you fail to integrate technology into your business, it might compromise your ability to compete in the market. Not only that, but it might also be more difficult to maintain and retain your customers.

In this section, I will explore the different ways that you can use technology to make your day-to-day business processes easier and more efficient.

Customer Relationship Management (CRM) Software

CRM stands for Customer Relationship Management. It is a term used to refer to the strategies, programs and practices your barber shop should implement to help you analyze and manage all your customers' data and interactions.

Any form of technology that you will use in your business will be for the benefit of your customers. If it makes your business operations easier to manage, it will help you focus on your customers. When your customers are happy, you can expect them to return and be loyal to you. But the question is, what is the role of a CRM in making your customers happy?

Customer Relationship Management systems are designed to help you manage customer data so you can study and analyze what they want out of your business. It will allow you to identify the services they prefer, and what they are not interested in. Once you know the services they are interested in, you can focus on improving them, so your customers will have a better experience in your barber shop as they treat themselves to the products and services you offer.

Here are examples of how your CRM can help in your barber shop:

- Organize customer information and contact details.
- Manage appointments to avoid double-booking.
- Set up reminders for upcoming appointments both for your barber shop and the customer.
- Deliver news about new products or services, promos, and discounts the barber shop is offering.
- Update customers about schedules and holidays that can affect business operations.

These are only some of the things CRMs help you with. It is important for you to choose the right system that suits the type of business processes your barber shop has.

Email Campaigns

As noted, emails are probably one of the best tools this digital age has given us. It is a great tool for your barber shop because it allows you to implement continuous marketing campaigns.

Of course, email campaigns are more than the newsletter or content that you send out to your customer mailing list. You must know what type of emails you will send so they may be translated into customer transactions. So how do you go about an email campaign? Here are the steps that you need to follow:

Get the email address of your customers. New customers should be asked to input their data, specifically their name and contact details.

Send a personalized email to every new customer. This welcome email is a great way to make customers feel they are welcome back into the barber shop, and that you remember the service you gave them.

Automate reminders for the customer. Men usually need to have their hair cut more often than women. You may want to send biweekly reminders for the next haircut or other service.

Send an email of appreciation for the visit. Deliver your message of thanks and feel free to include details about services or products the customers can use the next time they visit. To make it personal, you may want to include haircare tips for the customer.

Give coupons or discounts to customers. Send them to the customer to encourage them to visit your barber shop once more.

Feel free to keep doing this. Send biweekly emails so your customers will be reminded you are always available to provide your services when they need you the most.

Customer Rewards Program

A rewards program is a great way to encourage loyalty and continuous patronage from your customers. You will reward them for always prioritizing your barber shop for their haircare requirements.

Here are more tips that you may want to consider:

- Create different reward levels based on how many times the customer visits the barber shop.
- Give them an incentive to return. For instance, if they visit your shop within the next two weeks, they get a discount or a free product or service (e.g., free massage).
- Encourage them to bring a friend. A referral can come in the form of a discount or a free service.
- Come up with a stamp card that will give them a

reward after continuous patronage. For instance, after 10 cuts, they get the 11th for free. This stamp card also can be in the form of a mobile app for easier tracking.

When you are creating a loyalty program for your barber shop, it is very important to keep your customers in mind. After all, you want to create a program that will appeal to them.

Chapter 10 Questions

- **Do you have a system in place to monitor and track your customers?**

- **What is your goal for attracting and retaining customers?**

- **What customer rewards programs can you put in place to increase customer loyalty?**

Chapter 11: What's Next? Using Innovation to Grow Your Barber Shop

The key to keeping your barber shop above the competition is to commit to a constant state of evaluation. You must learn how to innovate. And basically, there is not real risk of barbering being replaced, not even through artificial intelligence (robots). Therefore, you need to look for ways to improve your barber shop. It may come in the form of a service or product upgrade, a renovation or a training program. These will help improve something in the business so you may increase productivity and profitability.

In this section, I will discuss how important it is to train your employees and how to go about the expansion of your barber shop.

Investing in Training Staff and Expanding Locations

The growth of your barber shop can be manifested in two ways: your staff and the actual shop. Each of these will require you to invest some money and time. Let us discuss why it is worth the investment.

Training Opportunities for Staff

Your barber shop primarily offers services to your customers. You need to make sure your staff is well-trained and able to provide the needs of your customers. To start with, you want to make sure your staff knows how to treat the customers right. Not only that, they also should be prepared in case one of your customers has a complaint. While there are naturally charming people, some of your employees might not be like that. There are people who are very talented in cutting hair but have poor customer relationship skills. You need to train them on how to handle different kinds of customers.

Apart from the customer service, you also should invest in training for their haircutting and styling skills. Even men have evolving hairstyles, and you want to make sure that your stylists can meet customer demands.

Whenever you have new programs or systems that need to be implemented, you want to invest in training your staff for these upgrades. This is how they will learn to use the programs and systems properly. It could take some time to get used to, so you want to give your staff enough training to make this possible.

Expanding Your Location

Another sign of a growing business is expansion. In your barber shop, it could mean renovating your current location or opening a new one in another community. Sometimes upgrading the current barber shop is enough because that would give your present customer base something new to experience. Opening another barber shop in another location could be profitable; however, I would ensure that the main location is profitable. Of course, this is easier said than done. There are a lot of pressing considerations when you invest in a new location. It is very costly, and you should practically start from scratch. You need to process a new set of documents, market your barber shop in the new community, and get the trust of the people in that neighborhood. You will be risking much, so you need to ensure your barber shop will be appealing for the new market you will target.

The Cost and Benefits in Expanding Your Business

The cost to expand your barber shop will depend on your needs. Try not to assume that you will be spending the same amount of money as when you opened your first barber shop. You can use it as a benchmark, but not a template.

First, the costs today may not be the same as before. Obviously, you need to hire a contractor to build your barber shop. The labor cost might be higher compared to the time you built your first shop. Should you decide to lease, those costs could be higher. Owning or leasing is a decision you would have to make.

You also should consider the new location where you will expand. Are the costs higher or lower in that neighborhood? Can you give the same price point as your first shop? That would really depend on what your customers can afford and what the competition in that area offers.

While this investment will put a dent in your finances, there are many benefits to expanding your operations in another location. You will be tapping into a new market, and that means more customers. If you can build an army of loyal customers, you can quickly double your profits. Although the overhead will increase, the potential to earn will also go up.

Another benefit you can expect is publicity. The opening of a barber shop creates noise that also can benefit your other establishment. As you advertise your new location, mention your other shop and that could give your sales a boost.

Of course, you should make sure your calculations will be done smartly and carefully. Although you will be spending, make sure that it will be less than your expected earnings. You need to work on the return of this new investment if you want to continue growing your barber shop.

Chapter 11 Questions

- How often do you evaluate your barber shop and its position of growth and expansion?

- Where is the ideal location to place and expand your barber shop?

- If you plan to expand, when do you plan to implement the expansion?

Conclusion

I believe barbering is a profession that is going to be around until the end of time. While the fundamentals and craft of barbering remain the same, how one attracts a customer is key. Today's customer is on the go and in a rush, for the most part. So, offering more timely services would attract the customer even more. We see this type of strategy with corporations that own barber shops as they offer various services to meet the customer's needs. I call this level of service a one-stop-shop business, and I see this expanding in the future. To be a one-stop-shop barber shop, you must offer what your customer needs. By doing so it would be an easier sale, but you must know your customers' habits, likes and dislikes. For example, you cannot offer high-end products to a moderately income-based clientele. So, first what I'm saying is, whatever you offer must be in alignment with and attractive to your target market. Second, you must be able to take a risk by introducing something new. Third, whatever you offer, make sure it is appealing to the eye. You want to offer your product on top of a China plate instead of a garbage can lid. Presentation is key in all types of sales.

As you work and grow your business, it is my hope that you utilize the material in this book. Barbering is a rewarding profession to be in, and there is an enormous opportunity to make a great deal of money. The success and direction of your barber shop is up to you. You are the captain of this ship! While I do not expect you to take away every piece of material in this book, the action steps below are paramount to the success of your business:

- Develop and execute a plan for your barber shop. Always have a plan in everything you do.
- Seek guidance on the things you don't understand.
- Do not spend every penny you make. Separate it for emergencies, your retirement, savings, and paying yourself.
- Always network, build business relationships and service your community.
- Always do the right thing and I dare you to do it right!

All the best in your future endeavors!

About the Author

A visionary who serves the community, Alan D. Benson is the founder and president of Benson Group, LLC, a company that positions individuals and companies to operate efficiently and effectively.

Alan is passionate about helping others discover their true potential. He believes every experience and job we have had in life helps to shape our identity, attitude, and journey in life; and that it is up to us to recognize the reasoning for those experiences, learn how to assemble them, and apply them to our purpose in life. This belief is his driving force in Benson Group, LLC's goal to equip individuals and companies to reach their true potential and business goals.

Alan earned a Bachelor of Science degree in Political Science and Master of Public Administration (MPA) degree from the University of Louisville. He later earned a Master of Business Administration (MBA) degree from Indiana University. He served in the United States Marine Corps Reserves and is a Persian Gulf War veteran. He is married to Dr. Debbie Benson and has a stepson, Landon Brewer, and twins, Hilton and Hayley Benson. He resides in Atlanta, GA.

References

https://www.entrepreneur.com/article/223126
http://www.investopedia.com/terms/m/marketing.asp
http://www.purelybranded.com/insights/the-four-ps-of-marketing/
http://smallbusiness.chron.com/market-barbershop-10568.html
https://www.sba.gov/blogs/sole-proprietorship-popular-business-structure-right-you
https://www.desk.com/success-center/customer-service
https://www.accenture.com/us-en/insight-digital-disconnect-customer-engagement
http://www.investopedia.com/terms/c/customer-service.asp
https://www.retailcustomerexperience.com/blogs/why-customer-service-and-branding-are-the-same-thing/
https://www.ballantine.com/3-reasons-why-a-customer-mailing-list-is-important/
http://smallbusiness.chron.com/build-customer-list-21992.html
http://www.bluefountainmedia.com/blog/direct-mail-marketing-and-email-marketing/
http://www.mastersofbarbering.com/blog/2012/02/07/how-to-be-a-barber-barbershop-customer-service-tips-part-4/
http://www.artofmanliness.com/2009/08/18/how-to-pick-a-barber/
https://www.standishsalongoods.com/masculine-barbershop-decor
http://www.ehow.com/how_10064334_decorate-barbershop.html
https://www.biznessapps.com/blog/why-every-hair-salon-and-barbershop-needs-a-business-app/
http://searchcrm.techtarget.com/definition/CRM
http://blog.marketo.com/2014/05/instagram-barbershops-and-the-power-of-continuous-

marketing.html
http://www.startabarbers.co.uk/expanding-
barber-shop-business.html
http://www.capitolhillseattle.com/2015/03/rudys-
barbershop-opening-on-15th-ave-e/comment-page-1/

Made in the USA
Columbia, SC
09 September 2022

66481112R00067